CONTENTMENT IN LIFE 03

Edited by

Becki Mee

First published in Great Britain in 1999 by
POETRY NOW
Remus House,
Coltsfoot Drive,
Woodston,
Peterborough, PE2 9JX
Telephone (01733) 898101
Fax (01733) 313524

HB ISBN 0 75430 759 X
SB ISBN 0 75430 760 3

FOREWORD

Although we are a nation of poets we are accused of not reading poetry, or buying poetry books. After many years of listening to the incessant gripes of poetry publishers, I can only assume that the books they publish, in general, are books that most people do not want to read.

Poetry should not be obscure, introverted, and as cryptic as a crossword puzzle: it is the poet's duty to reach out and embrace the world.

The world owes the poet nothing and we should not be expected to dig and delve into a rambling discourse searching for some inner meaning.

The reason we write poetry (and almost all of us do) is because we want to communicate: an ideal; an idea; or a specific feeling. Poetry is as essential in communication, as a letter; a radio; a telephone, and the main criteria for selecting the poems in this anthology is very simple: they communicate.

CONTENTS

FATHER'S LOT

Many fathers, these days, are out of work
The paternal instinct, they cannot shirk
Left at home, to deal with the kids
Is a real opener, for their eyelids
Cooking dinners, feeding faces
Putting children, in their places
Washing machines, iron, microwave oven
What a mess, better get glove on
Clean up more mess, bread, Marmite
Before the lady, comes home, tonight
Hoover, dust, wash up, mow the lawn
Quickly open, carrots, sweetcorn
Prepare a hot sumptuous dinner
For the working lady, now breadwinner
Smile as she asks, what she's got
Role reversal, a modern father's lot.

Danny Coleman

DAD

Memories -
Now fading of a person long ago
I never truly knew him,
But I know he loved me so
I was but just a little girl
When my father passed away
It never once occurred to me
He wasn't there to stay
I know it's no good wishing
For times we never had
Just remember all you lucky ones
Appreciate your dad.

F M Wilkinson

UNTITLED

When I was five you came into my life,
The dad I never had.

You cared,
You loved,
You've supported me through,
Anything I've ever wanted to do.

Twenty years on our bond is still strong.

I only have to ask and you're here in a flash.

Now baby-sitting grandchildren,
doing my jobs.
Picking me up or dropping me off.

It's never a bother you just give a big smile -

You're one in a million and do it with style.

So Dad - what more is there to say,
Just that I love you more every day!

Emma Morton

A POEM ON HIS DAY

So many fine days that I've had 'cross the years'
But each year there's one that stands out.
To focus and show just a hint of my love
And that's what this day is about.

There's never a normal day ever goes by
Without one small thought for my dad,
But only on this day I take the time out
To thank him for times that we had.

And each Father's Day kept, as times glide on past,
As far as my mem'ry can see,
Now strengthens the tie that unites us as one
And brings home his presence to me.

I'll always hold dear, on this day every year,
The love that a few words can show
For Dad my old mate, who died one night quite late,
Just eighteen years one month ago.

T J Martin

MY FATHER

I look up to my father
Who has taught me all I know
To look on the bright side
When if ever I feel low

To be truthful and straight
In all my dealings
In whatever job I do
I don't have to be a doctor
Or a solicitor or priest

But whatever job I'm suited to
My father's words I'll treasure
In any job I do
So respect your father
And remember his words of advice
And if ever you have a child of your own
You can give him the same advice.

Mary M Jones

FATHER

The tiny child is sleeping
Outside a storm is brewing
Time is passing
But this place is safe

I watch the child sleep
Watch the world sleep
This is my moment
When the sky is dark
And I am alone in a sleeping world

In the light of morning
My world is monochrome
Logical
I bear it on my shoulders
With emotions locked up safe
Securely fastened
Hidden in a box

But night has fallen
And the world is different
It is a world of ghosts
Where spirits and demons whisper
Loudly in the silent night
Thoughts have replaced actions
Scared and unsure
I have seen the future
Have witnessed suffering and death

I weep for the memory of my own father
For the day when I am a memory
A faded photograph
In the bottom of a drawer

I wait for sunrise.

Judith Logan

Is Daddy Really Fun?

My daddy is so much fun,
He seems to brighten up everyone,
He always laughs even when he's sad,
He laughs at us for being so bad,
He tells me off when he was small,
Of how he pushed his dad to make him fall.

My daddy is so much fun,
He seems to brighten up everyone,
Until he tells us what jobs there are,
Like feed the dog or wash the car.

My daddy is so much fun,
He mostly brightens everyone,
But when I'm really down,
I don't want any jobs around.

David Mitchell (12)

ABSENT FATHERS

I wonder who my father was?
I wish I'd had a Dad!
Someone to teach me how to shave,
and love me when I'm sad.
Someone to share the manly things,
that women don't allow,
To share the conversation points,
that only a man would know.

Yet as I watch the other dads,
It all seems rather odd.
I notice that they don't spend time,
the way I thought they would.
They always seem to be away,
Or busy on a call.
My friends don't seem to get the chance,
To be with Dad at all!

I wonder if I missed that much?
My mum was always there!
She always did the best she could,
She always seemed to care.
I guess I'd better not complain,
There's no need to be sad.
Perhaps it isn't all that tough,
To never know your Dad!

Tony Harris

QUESTIONS TO DAD

How long did you stay, initially, after I was born?
A week, a few months; longer?
Only you can say, now that mother's gone.
How often did you visit?
Could I count the times on both hands; or less?
Or should I calculate the hours?

I did well with my past education,
and my present profession is progressing well.
Did you know that? Do you even care?
A few boyfriends have come and gone.
All older; query wiser? Did you know any of them?
I got married, you turned up, made me cry; why?

You have other children, my half-brothers and sisters.
Questions? I'm sure they have many of their own.
But this is about me; for me.
Did you really think that a little money here,
or a gift there, would make me love you?
Promising to remember me in your will,
would that endear me to you now?

When I yearned for you to show me love,
it was nowhere to be seen.
Now retirement awaits you, around the corner,
you wish for me to show you love.
What do you think my answer to you would be?
Questions to Dad. Answers not required. Too late.

Naomi Donegan

DAD'S THREE BEST FRIENDS

Arch supports in laced up boots,
Warm flannel shirts and navy suits,
Fleecy long johns over knee length socks,
Work worn hands as hard as rocks.
Up early each day, round at the stable,
Horse in the shafts to put food on the table.
Whatever the weather you could always rely
On potato or apple for your favourite pie.

An empty cart at the end of the day -
'Right Bob, home' was all dad had to say.
Horse standing still, head hanging low,
Back at the stable, nowhere to go.
Dad, head on chest, having a nap,
Never dislodging his worn cloth cap.

Many years have passed and I must confess
I have never forgotten Bob, Prince and Jess -
Those three gentle giants with such tender ways
Will live in my heart for the rest of my days.
I know dad is happy, no more to roam -
His three friends are with him; they're safely home.

Mary Davies

THE SHED

Every dad must have his shed,
a quiet retreat to sort out his head,
a place to call his own private, one-man club,
just down the garden from the family hub,
away from the wife, kids, mother-in-law,
where he can hammer, screw and saw.

Every dad must have his shed,
a quiet retreat to sort out his head,
a place to give his problems an outing,
without the hysterics, the screaming, the shouting,
away from the stress of modern living,
the pressure cooker that's unforgiving.

Every dad must have his shed,
a quiet retreat to sort out his head,
a place he can go to rejuvenate,
to face again his chosen fate,
that thankless role of father figure,
with a renewed strength and vigour.

Michael Hutchins

DAD THE LAD

My father was a family man
A family in Ireland, two in Japan
I've brothers and sisters all over the place
Some I do know, most I can't trace

He's now turning ninety and getting quite low
The last one he married he don't even know
The wives got the message he's not going to mend
They arrived in bus loads to be in at the end

There will be tears at the funeral, fun with the will
All those young wives who weren't on the pill
There's a couple of kids with a very young mum
I'm beginning to think, like father like son.

Robert Browne

FATHERHOOD

Fathers, we need them quite a lot,
Without them, there is no tiny tot,
A daughter, to show to the world with pride,
A son, a junior version to keep alongside.

The hustle and bustle, of a busy day,
The time taken to earn enough pay,
Fitting in everything and seeing the children too,
Seems occasionally, almost impossible to do.

Playing football, children's parties and having fun,
Luckily fathers don't often do, the 'school run'.
Homework; now there is something for Father to do,
Changing in time, to chauffeur too!

The different friends, now possible partners too,
For fathers to meet, view and approve too?
Holiday; marriage and mortgage, which will it be,
Father just has to wait; patiently.

Children really do grow up fast,
They think they have got it right at last.
The big day and Father glows with pride,
His child has a partner by their side.

Father watches the lifecycle start anew,
Watches to see what his child will do.
A problem, a glitch, Father looks on in despair,
What can he do to clear the air.

Time marches on, Father watches a new life unfold,
Horror of horrors, surely he is not getting old.
Never! Just wiser with experience to pass on,
Then a slight blur - is he father or son.

Patricia Curnow

FATHERS

Loving, caring
giving, sharing
helping, showing
teaching, knowing.

A father is but all these things
he's so much more as well.
He'll guide you, love you, teach
you, hold you,
your secrets he won't tell.

His job involves so many things,
he's busy all day long,
making sure you've got all you need,
and showing you right from wrong.

So love your father with all your heart
he's someone to treasure always,
he'll give you so much in your life
he'll do it in so many ways.

L Werney

HAPPY FATHER'S DAY

Happy Father's Day dear Dad
or should I say Robson Green
Well that's who the kids
say you look like on old
photos they have seen.

They think you look like a film star
or someone off the telly
I used to tell my friends
my dad looks like Gene Kelly.

Remember when I wouldn't go to school
I made such a song and dance
You put me over your shoulders
and took me through the boys' entrance.

When my leg got stuck in Grainger's fence
you weren't very pleased
Because you had to chop it down
so that I could be released.

Then when I grew up and
I got married in style
I'm glad you were there
to walk me down the aisle.

You've been the best father
anyone could ever have had
You loved us and cared for us
Happy Father's Day dear Dad.

Angela Asher

To Daddy

Is it really a year since you went away?
A year since I last saw you asleep in your cosy bed
so peaceful with your tender eyes closed for the very last time.
A whole year since you took me in your arms for a loving hug
when I came to see you and Mum in your warm home.

You didn't want to leave us
You said so many times
But in the end you went quietly
without a fuss.

I can't believe I shall not ever see you again
Never touch your strong arms
or hear your soft voice.
Never walk with you through town, stopping to greet the many folk
you knew and loved.
You always had a good word for everyone
and were rightly loved by them all
in return.

I miss you so much, Daddy
but I try not to be sad
because you always taught me to appreciate all the love we had.

You were so brave
so courageous and thoughtful
always a smile on your face
giving love right to the end.

And now I have Lee
My precious new grandson.
I wish you'd seen him born
But though he'll not meet his great-grandad
I'll tell him all about you
So that your love and life goes on and on.

I can't believe it's a year
since you last said you love me
but I'll try to follow your example,
as I know you'd want me to do
and take care of dear Mummy
and treasure life the way that you did.

Thank you for being my Daddy
I'm still my Daddy's girl
And still I can't believe it.
Is it really a year since you went away?

Suzanne Arnold

A FATHER'S DREAM

I remember as a boy
Playing football in the park,
We'd go there in the morning
Come home when it got dark,
Having fun with my best friends
For whom I cared so much,
I hardly ever see them now
Somehow we just lost touch,
I dreamed I'd play for Liverpool
The other's Manchester United,
But life did not work out as planned
And all our dreams were blighted,
Life goes on, dreams passed us by
And we've reached a certain age,
Now that dream will never be
We're trapped in life's big cage,
Most of us are fathers now
With children of our own,
Can the dream be realised
When our kids have grown?
My son could play for England
If I teach him right,
Not to drink, not to smoke
And don't stay out all night,
I'll give him all the discipline
That I never had,
'Cause he's got something that I missed
In me, a caring dad,

I love my son with all the love
That a father feels inside,
And as he's growing older
I'll instil a sense of pride,
I hope that when he's older
He's in a football team,
I hope he plays for England
And realise his father's dream.

Richard Leach

CHILD'S SONG

Oh where is my father?
He who should dandle me by still waters,
Lift me and carry me on rough shoulders,
Tease me with money, hard-earned and welcome,
Be the perfect model in my role.

Oh where is my father?
Sounding like teddy bears,
Smelling of tobacco,
Feeling like hedgehogs,
And tasting of beer.

Oh where is my father?
Nurturing,
Providing,
Protecting
And saving.

Oh where is my father?
The man who created me,
Modelled me,
Lifted me,
Kissed me

And died.

Veronica Butcher

DAD

Of all the memories I recall
Dad stood out amongst them all.
In strong arms he'd lift me high
I thought that I could reach the sky.
We'd play football down at the park
run and race till nearly dark.

Friday night he'd bring home treats,
pennies and large coloured sweets.
When my bike I learned to ride
he was there right by my side.

My schooldays were hard for me
I doubted my ability.
I told him of my inner fear,
could I succeed in my career?

Now I am a man full grown
with two young children of my own.
A little older turning grey,
happily with them he'll play.

The years have flown and yet I'm glad
for he will always be
My Dad!

Sheila Rowark

DAD

In our family my dad is the clever parrot,
a kind canary,
a sleeping sloth,
he's a hairless tower of knowledge,
a happy giraffe,
a lazy cuckoo,
he makes me laugh,
but sometimes when Dad is a bit irritated
he turns into . . .
a leave-me-alone
a floppy ragdoll,
a shut the door,
a swarm of bees,
when Dad's like this we leave him alone,
because he is the monster whose name is
unknown!

Nicola Matthews (12)

DREAMSCAPE

There's a place I go to,
It's off the beaten track -
It's quite easy getting there,
Not so simple coming back!

It's a place not far from me
Where I leave the world behind -
There's no pain or animosity
And it's with me all the time.

It's a place where I can feel at home,
Because it lies at the heart of me -
I wish I could stay and never roam,
But how can I - it's only a fantasy . . .

Steve Utting

ME SITTING ON THE BEACH

The lovely yellow sand,
Hear the waves crashing against the rocks,
Hear the birds making noises in the sky,
Touching the nice, smooth, yellow sand,
It is soft and slimy,
See the dogs running,
See the people surfing on the nice blue sea,
Feel the warmth from the sun
And also can feel the breeze blowing the sand in my face.

Emma Sloan (12)

TALLY RACE '98

The Fairway buoy is where we're to be -
My Pico and me, two miles out to sea.
A little dot, to you and me,
Just two miles out to sea.

Off I go, I'm in the lead -
Tacking the wind and riding the waves,
My boat sings sweetly to me,
Whilst we're two miles out to sea.

The Fairway buoy, from the sea -
Is bigger, than you or me.
Round I go in the lead,
Everyone chasing me,
Two miles out to sea.

Suddenly the waves are gone,
They have gone from under me.
Bang - I went into the sea,
Now the boat is on top of me,
But for how long, until I'm free?
Only the waves know that they are stopping me,
Oh how that sea is cruel to me.

Gemma Steele (12)

THE BEACH

The blue waves crash upon the open shore.
The white foam bubbles and then is no more.
The blazing sun masquerades its beams of light,
Whilst shadows of birds are taking their flight.
Prints once belonging to feet now belong to the sea.
The beach is now peaceful, lonely but free.
The seagulls squawk their last goodbyes,
As the sun goes down and finally dies.

Laura Attipoe

A PLACE FOR ANGELS

What can I see beyond these eyes
As my soul discards its earthly ties?
My soul transported to paradise?
A heavenly fluttering fills the air
No more anguish, pain or despair.
Beauty seeps from its every pore
My earthly body hits the floor.
Arms outstretched you beckon me
An engulfing light envelops me.
I've always felt you at my side
As you join me on heaven's ride.
Your golden light protects my soul
As we reach heaven's door.
Beauty words could not describe
As your light retreats from my side.
Oceans of turquoise, fields of dew
A fluttering of clouds, sky a piercing blue.
An angel stands erect and proud
My soul has left its earthly shroud.
I've finally reached my heavenly retreat
As I claim my golden seat.

Christian Jones (15)

SENSING A SPECIAL PLACE

The time is near for it to come,
But it seems to find it funny,
To stay inside. To act so dumb,
It's in the womb inside her tummy.

For nine months it's lived in total bliss,
No worries about what's for dinner,
It could be chips or even fish,
Either way it is the winner.

It's nearly time for bed right now,
But suddenly it started up,
Strong and big contractions,
They send her off to give it up.

The head is coming, it's all out,
They turn the shoulders to help it,
She's pushing and shouting,
Out it comes and then they wrap it.

It's a baby girl and full of joy,
When it's time to feed she'll let you know,
Dirty nappies are lots of fun,
Still out of the hospital they will come.

Sera-Jean Glover

CHURCH

The church,
the tranquil shelter of
joy and despair,
the ceilings decked with
cherubs smiling down at
you with their sorrowful
yet congratulating stares.

The place where I
watched my friend being
carried up in a solid oak
box will always sustain
a special place in my heart.

Luke Finn (13)

THE BEACH

A gush of wind,
Flew through my hair,
Making it scatter, everywhere.

The sounds of waves,
Quickly crashing,
People running, and start splashing.

The sun blazing,
Upon the crowd,
That played, and laughed extremely loud.

So suddenly,
People moved on,
Back to their cars, the sun had gone.

Clouds then gathered,
The tide rushed in,
The sky is darkening, the moon is coming.

Sam Swain (13)

THE SUNSET

One morning I woke up,
got up and got ready
to go to the beach
with my family.
We spent all day there
making sandcastles,
it was a fun day out.
At about 8pm it was
time to go home when
I noticed the sun setting.
The sun rippled over the
sea, the sun slowly vanished,
then it was about 10pm so
we had to go home.

David Maxfield (13)

THE GRAVEYARD

The graveyard,
No matter what the weather
Dark and gloomy
I enter
Feelings of sadness enveloping my mind.

Rows of gravestones,
Different shapes and sizes
But all the same dull grey,
Worn edges
Casting misty shadows on the cold, hard ground.

A separate world
Cut off from civilisation, from happiness,
Sad and solitary.
Trees sway in the breeze,
Branches hung heavy in despair.

Memories of the dead,
Peaceful silence,
The scent of flowers lingers in the air.
A place to reflect,
Remember loved ones that have passed through, undisturbed.

Spirits lift,
Colours return as the light breaks through.
The refreshing rain washes away the sadness,
A single bird song invades the silence,
Satisfied I return to the living world.

Janine Lumley (14)

BY AN ITALIAN SHORE

Golden warmth
All-pervading, glowing, driving out the chill from within,
Seeping through the soles of my feet.

Tiny grains,
Sand-sharp, bone white,
Grazing the spaces between my toes.

Silver ripples,
Bath-warm, sparkling, murmuring,
Fluttering out to the edge of my vision (to eternal shores?)

A shell,
Small, pointed, smooth and pink,
Scuttles away from my reaching hand
On tiny pincer feet.

Never before
Have I felt this warmth,
This all-embracing, gentle heat.

Never before
Have I seen these sights,
Heard these sounds.

Perhaps I will come this way again

In memory.

Liz Piper

EGYPT

Egypt it is hot
Full of beauty spots
Sandy deserts
Reminds you of evening desserts
Breath taking sights, oh what a flight
With a blanket of sand
Which falls on your hand
A dazzling light
Refreshes in bright

Egypt is full of dates
Surprises you with blind dates
Romantic bumpy rides
With lots of pride
Sun goes down at height
Sizzling heat at night
Splendid by the warm colours gay
Spreading throughout the day
All eyes twinkle with its lash
Scoops of wonder in a flash

Egypt is a dream feature
Layered with exotic creatures
Polished in historical atmosphere
Dry lands surrounded by trees
Flowing gently in the morning breeze
Air full of sparkling fumes
White clouds covered by city looms
Glowing in and out colours are brown
Steadily put on like a golden crown
Egypt it is an angel delight
Specially in the moonlight

Rabina Ali (14)

SENSING A SPECIAL PLACE
(The countryside)

A winding pathway draws me on,
a beautiful chorus at the break of dawn.
Dew on the daisies
at the side of the lake.
Robin sits ready,
his breakfast to take.

Elegant lilies on the water poised,
bees are humming with summer noise.
Whistling warmth of the summer breeze,
shadows and colours through the trees.
Violets and roses capture the air,
almost whispering summer's here!

Jacqueline Brown

BLACK DOG

We are not strangers now, black dog.
Others have known you too: slinking
From the shadows, snuffling and thin,
Persistent in your following.
Trotting along behind, biding
Your time, you are prepared to wait
To seize your opportunity -
Cleverly you ingratiate
Susceptible hearts, guileless minds.

Shouting never frightened you or
The hex sign. Closing eyes is fine
Until, opening them once more,
Finds you still here. Deep breathing calms
The mind, but then you sit and whine -
Nothing I do makes you disappear.

So finally the bottom line
Is knowing that you're here to stay -
Best to ignore you, come what may.

Each cunning sidelong glance reveals
You resting, head on paws today,
Or idly sitting scratching fleas -
Each time you're always watching me
With eyes half shut, never asleep:
Unwanted friend waits patiently.

Then sometimes, with the longer days,
You leave, abruptly disappear,
And I relax in summer's sun
And savour this changed atmosphere.
Yet still I know it cannot last
'Though I've escaped from time to time,
You'll suddenly appear, black dog,
And nuzzle me as if you're mine.

In autumn, with the falling leaves,
You come. When copper sun rests on
The trees I see you gliding through
The wood; knowing, with summer gone
You'll seek me out - it's understood.

Patrick Osada

THE MONTH OF MAY

What a lovely time of year
Is the month of May,
When the countryside is refreshed
And in the meadows lambs play.

The trees are dressed
In their gowns of green lace
And the world seems a brighter
And happier place.
The hedgerows and gardens
With blossoms abound,
And it's good to get away
From the bustle of the town.

So for a while leave behind the TV
And make it a duty,
Go and feast your eyes
On this God-given beauty;
Then when winter returns
With its cold dreary days,
We'll have beautiful memories,
For which to give God the praise.

Margaret Hodges

BLUE WIND IN AFRICA
(To Linda)

Calm seas of utter restfulness
and peace within the storm
the clanging of the rope against the mast
the slapping of the waves against the hull
the gulls shriek high and lift those spirits to the sky . . .

'Sail on around, not through the eye but on,
around and round . . .
Until all passes into inconsequence . . . '

Glistening sails stand proud against the rays of sun
and billow out the azure light of dreams serene
Blue winds blow in from Africa
Where we have been in times of innocence
When we knew not of troubles,
When we were babes as yet unborn to strife and consequence
Afloat in plains of Serengeti wonder
Blue Wind in Africa; our Hope, our Dream, our Future yet to come . . .

Sandra Finch

TRANSFIGURATION

When the fire blazed fierce
just before it died,
we'd sit, making pictures.
Elbows on knees,
I'd watch her gazing into space.
Shadows soft as moss
blurred shabby corners,
cast lustre over bloom,
and on the overmantel
gilt cherubs flew,
fat and laughing.
She'd poke the coals and
embers crashed and fell
upon themselves,
crackling and hissing
sending showers of sparks
dancing like fireflies
up the chimney
leaving a centre,
black and scarlet.
A cavern of flames
and ash, transformed to
dragons, witches, unicorns.
Shadows flickering,
our heads together,
never so close.

And when her coffin slid away
and curtains closed,
I thought of her, alone
and incandescent,
like a sunburst.

Sylvie Farquhar

JESS

As I gaze upon your face
Into eyes of deepest blue,
Words cannot express
The love I feel for you
As I gently hold you close
In the circle of my arms.
My joy is now complete
As I hold you safe and warm,
For you've enriched my life
With so much happiness.
Thank you, my grand-daughter,
My lovely little Jess.

Vi Fazackerley

STARDUST

For every teardrop that falls in the snow
For all the cries he hears you know
For all the hearts broken in two
The magic of stardust is sprinkled on you

Magical stardust is sprinkled each day
Tiniest grains of love floating our way
Some reach the birds winging above
Some to the children whose birth brings such love

Just for a second when love fills your heart
Be sure that the stardust has reached its mark
Through the magic of time sweetest love unfolds
The longings of lovers their bodies to hold

From the laughter of children whilst at their play
On a lifetime's journey until the end of our day
Wind blows harder so far and wide
Nothing and no one from the stardust can hide

Such a small bag of stardust, its magic will fall
From God's heaven to reach us all.

Susan E Roffey

THE SEA

Merciless sea in thy fury,
Pounding the rocks in violent rage,
Shipwrecks and bodies, your victims you hide
In murky grey waters, forever entombed.

Howling winds pierce jet-black skies,
Giant waves heave in turbulent swell,
A helpless lifeboat clings to life,
Struggling to conquer the mighty sea.

Shrouded by saffron clouds, streaky black,
The raging storm relentlessly battles on,
On bended knee, man alone may plead,
His voice engulfed by a force unknown.

Daybreak, the grim aftermath of destruction,
The silent shudder of death, lingers
Over an icy corpse in an ocean grave,
A brave man, devoured by the hand of fate.

Diana Frewin

HOW

Miracles you say - what nonsense, how sad.
And a God who cares - you must be mad!
And yet . . . and yet . . . it would explain,
How the universe began, without the aid of mortal man.

Sun, moon and stars, how formed in space,
And Earth produce the human race.
Without a God how could this be,
From nothingness came you and me?

How wind and water, fire and air,
Without which life would disappear,
Supports the life they say began
In heavenly places through God's Son.

How everything has shape and form,
And even in the fiercest storm,
The awesome sight can touch the soul,
As lightnings flash and thunders roll.

How from dead seed life springs anew,
Flowers and shrubs and ripe fruits too.
In this same way the Bible has said,
Jesus Christ arose from the dead.

A new day is dawning; some say it's begun.
Everyone hopes for a better world to come.
So, how can we know what we should believe?
God's word is clear: 'Ask, and you shall receive.'

Margaret Godliman

GRANDMA

She was born in December 1910,
times were hard in Britain then.

She grew up knowing just one town,
struggling through life's ups and downs.

As an adult she worked on the land,
work and survival went hand in hand.

She was so proud of her many memories,
pre-war Britain and those young evacuees!

She married her first love back in 1932,
so lucky in love, she found something true.

She gave birth soon after to just the one,
this turned out to be my dear old mum.

Independence was with her until the end,
my Grandma, my inspiration, my friend.

Debra Neale

DIRECTIONS

Dawning sunrays greet with golden welcome,
Flickering through the leaves of the waymark tree.
So, pilgrim, begin your lifequest journey.
Take one last look at the cold blue sea.
Go to the distant snow-peaked mountain.
Fill your lungs with the scent of wild thyme.
Look eastwards cross the fertile valley.
The emerald hill is the one you must climb.
Down to the island of the crystal lake,
See where duck and geese construct their nest.
On to the far off silver birch spinney,
Watch butterflies play whilst you rest.
Continue to the ancient dark oak forest,
Amongst ferns and pimpernels you spend the night.
Badger creeps, hedgehog snorts as you slumber,
Awaiting the sun's welcoming light.
Moonbeams dance like flickering fairies,
Dark shows the Dog Star and the Plough.
Night appears in such wondrous splendour.
To its creator, I can only bow.
Towards the headwaters of the whistling river,
The otter shyly watches from bubbling streams,
A creation of some grand plan dreams.
The path by wild honeysuckle is yours,
It leads to where violets and cornflower grow.
Admire the red poppies and purple campions,
Streamlets appear and vanish, where no-one knows.
You will see the Temple of All Knowledge,
And breathe the early morning air so clear.
Learn to appreciate all that surrounds you.
Discover why I love Planet Earth so dear.

B L Haswell

PEDAL POWER

My husband loves to ride his bike,
He says it keeps him fit,
Winter, summer, rain or shine,
He doesn't mind a bit.

In fact, when John's confined indoors,
Which happens very rarely,
His instinct is to blame the fates
For treating him unfairly.

One day a week he rides with *twerps* -
'*The Wednesday Expedition*
For Retired Persons', all of whom
Like 'keeping in condition'.

The riders once were young and spry
And speed was of importance;
What mattered was to finish first -
In theory, by some distance.

But now that they are pensioners
On daily medication
They've had to moderate their goals
To suit the situation.

Yet goals remain. Oh yes indeed!
The most exhausting projects -
The best by far took place last year,
The '*drug-assisted hundred*'.

It didn't make the newspapers,
The drugs involved were legal,
But John came home 'as proud as Punch'
And every inch as regal.

Sheila Burnett

FROM WHERE I STAND V

The calming sea at night
A blanket upon the fire within
No crashing stones
But still the screeching sounds
From where I stand
The ships with no cargo
Illuminate the arcing bay
There are senses within blackness
That only the sea can touch

Warren Brown

BORN AGAIN

Next time
I will be a snake,
exotic, clothed
in burnished gold and black
slithering sinuously into rooms
coiling myself round arms
and legs at untamed parties.
Given to intrigue and subtle
shedding of skins when things get hot,
I will be called
Snake-woman and everyone will admire
my black forked tongue.
In the cool of dark night
I will lie under verandahs
with my coiled snake-lovers
sensuous, breathing passion.

More probable - a sheep
fat and woolly, I will amble,
clumsy and good-natured,
plain-faced, bemused;
no one will name me.
Wider than tall, growing
knitwear on my back
and warm winter coats
will be a duty.
None too bright, but useful
will be the verdict
and I will shuffle, stout and slow
with other sheep - too many
for me to talk of numbers -
identical, assuming I am
the clever shepherd's favourite.

Fay Emerson

GEORGE

You were all I ever wanted
and everything I knew I could never have;
You were every schoolgirl's dream,
every woman's theme . . .
Multitudes loved you
but none as much as me;
others got married and had families,
only I was left hanging on the tree . . .
You were the irreplaceable demi-god
(by anyone's standards):
How could my heart ever trade you
for someone similar
when you were
the most unique entity
of the 20th century?
. . . You have always been my man;
it is a tragedy of human existence
that God could never do arithmetic
. . .and an even greater personal tragedy
that *I* now *can.*

Tricia Nolan

LONELY

Lonely inside the feelings are trapped
No one to talk to I'm all alone
My head spins with emotions
Each one waiting to burst.

Outside is clear and bright
I stay in fearing the unknown
Only the four walls surrounding keep me
I stay in hiding.

Someone come and set me free
I send out a message
The answers just bounce off the walls
I still sit waiting to be relieved
I still sit in my own world.

How I long to have a clear mind
But what you did to me made me blind
I cannot see past my window
Where a world waits to be filled.

How long do I have to wait
For someone to come
Maybe a day
Maybe forever
Until then my four walls keep me safe.

J L Hammond

MOBILE PHONE/MOBILE HOME

A business man on a mobile phone,
stands near to a man who has no home,
with a heap of dirty rags,
and a carrier bag
with all his possessions within.

What's the difference between each man,
nothing besides a plan for his life,
one ended up with money,
the other's life is far from sunny,
and we, who are we,
we are all onlookers in-between.

Hazel-Ann Knight

SOMETHING I ATE

Forever I must contemplate,
my health and work and motivate,
My words could be preponderate,
to those that I infatuate,
so why I just procrastinate,
is one thing I can't vindicate,
My dreams they are, inordinate,
for lack of drive I generate,
I really must accentuate,
potentially I'm profligate,
Myself I just infuriate,
assume that this must be my fate.

Suzan Legge

BLUEBELL WALK

We walked
We talked
To share your memory
And then your spirit
Began to overflow
For this is love
The music gently overflows
And I a bluebell prince

That purple bluey rose
That glows
The bluebell show
A mist you would think
Is the beauty love
The snow

Then you
The rising rose
I kneel to say
My princess
This is the love I feel
This is the love I reveal

Denis Manley

MY YEAR TWO THOUSAND

The year two thousand will soon be with us
another year to look ahead
to think of all the years gone past
and realise they went so fast.

So what is left must be well used
good health maintained, faith renewed.
For life is for living, learning and giving
new places to see, new people to meet
each day a new day, a new dawn to greet.

And now a new millennium to urge us all along
to greater achievements and to right all our wrongs
not only for ourselves but also for others
so the world will know we really are brothers
regardless of country, religion or colour
we can all learn to live and love one another.

Mary Kinney

MY BELIEF

Sometimes I find life confusing
I look around and see beliefs
Some are righteous and abide by the rules
Hoping for reward, if they concede.

Some people live for the moment
With barely time to think
And little time spent worrying
Just trusting their instinct.

Perhaps this is the way to live
Non-judgmental, with an open mind
Listening to one's inner voice
And *connecting* with humankind.

Myself, I am confused
For tradition, rules and fear
Feel unnatural and controlling
And almost too much to bear.

For each person is an individual
Though some cling to mass identities
And as a mass they speak as one
Combining responsibilities.

Sooner or later the search will begin
For personal authenticity
And the best tribute we can give
Is to respect our own individuality.

I feel, after much searching
I will allow myself to just *be*
And the best way to honour my existence
Is to believe in *me*.

To listen to my *free* spirit
To allow myself to *feel*
This, I believe, is the greatest compliment
To the energy that makes me real.

Julie Wilkins

GOOD
POEM

THE CRITERION HOTEL, AND SAM

Gone are the days of the market -
And the bar, known as the 'Back of the Cri'
Where drinks would be sold,
Whilst tales would be told, and arguments . . . should anyone lie;
      The sales were held each Saturday morning -
Within the sight of the 'Old Town Hall Clock'
Those being sold were cattle and pigs,
There were times, maybe the odd horse . . . they were usually old,
If not, some 'dodge' . . . maybe 'The' W'rigs.
      Now! There once was a time a' thought I'd a find
'In a real owd 'Irish Gig' -
But sad to say . . . It was rotting away,
But somehow a buyer was found.
      There was 'Sam,' he was one of the regulars,
Both for buying and selling, the same,
A fine jolly fellow . . . not at all 'moody' -
But I'm damned if I can think of his name;
He would stand you a pint if you traded -
With anything that he had sold,
But anything that he had bought from you,
He'd demand . . .'Gi'me a bit o' luck! Summut t'fold'
      But Sam was a real decent fellow,
You'd find in the 'Back of the Cri'
Where he'd stand you a pint . . .
If he had to,
But the reason he would always ask . . . Why?
Now Sam is no longer a 'dealer,'
Gone too is the pub known by the name of 'The Cri'
Whilst those whom shared tales, whilst drinking with Sam,
If still here today -
Will all know the reason, and why.

Leslie F Dukes

ONE FACE AMONG MANY

I view two hundred faces
Within my working day.
Some are young and beautiful,
Others are crowned with grey.

I pity those employees
On the production line.
I wish that I could help them,
But that's no task of mine.

I'm sure I would lose my job
If I gave them a hand.
I have to be impartial;
The workers understand.

I know they talk about me,
I've seen them point and stare.
Some of them will smile at me,
While others simply glare.

At every Christmas party,
Nobody speaks to me.
I am just a 'wallflower'
Beside the Christmas tree.

But yearly, on New Year's Eve,
The night-shift stand round me.
When they hear the midnight chime
Their faces grin with glee.

If I were to smile at them
The staff would die of shock.
They are made of flesh and blood
But I'm the factory clock.

James Hoey

DEATH OF A FOX

Sweet, sweet little fox, wandering unawares,
Through poppies - little warning signs,
Painted blood red with tears.
Sweet, sweet little fox, with your fire coloured coat,
If only you knew that the hounds
Were coming for your throat.
Sweet, sweet little fox, basking in the sun,
There's a blood splattered sunrise shining on you -
If only you could see the sun.
Sweet, sweet little fox, hears the gunshot boom,
Takes no notice, doesn't know that
He'll have company soon.
Sweet, sweet little fox, sees the men on horses,
Runs to save his little life,
While flowers close in mourning.
Sweet, sweet little fox, sees the day moon high above,
Wishes he could be up there,
As barking knives the chilly air.
Sweet, sweet little fox, bounds across the grasses,
Hopes the dogs aren't after him,
Stops to let them pass him.
Sweet, sweet little fox, launched upon by the dogs,
Say one last prayer for the little fox,
For il est mort.

Rebecca Swan

TEMPUS OMNIA REVELAT

Torment, anguish, decision or not,
Which way to go I do not understand.
Why decide? Just live and see
My heart says home, my mind says stay.

Torment, anguish, decision I have made
Home to heaven, safe, secure, happy.
Dread, worry, how will they respond?
Explosion, anger, frustration, they calm.

Torment, anger, decision or not
Which way to go, I do not understand
Anger, love, calm, frustration, how do I know which way to go?
Tempus Omnia Revelat

Time reveals all

Louise C Wilson (19)

A SIMPLE MEAL

If I had to choose just one meal that was to be my last,
One I've enjoyed in days that are long gone, and sadly, past,
I think it would be one I had whilst on the Isle of Man.
I was on holiday there and getting a beautiful tan,
The weather was glorious - just right for our Gold Star motorbike,
Just sunshine all day, no breeze, even for the likes of a child's kite.
We'd rode all afternoon and so were now ready for a really tasty meal,
Something a bit special, but not costing a great deal.
Then, round a bend, a lean-to we saw
Covered only by fishermen's nets - we felt we could do with more!
But we were hungry, so at the cheap wooden table we both sat
And we were made really welcome - the owner coming over for a
                                        friendly chat.
We were offered bread and real butter, freshly pulled lettuce and mugs
                                        of sweet tea,
But best of all - boiled lobster - straight from the sea!
I still remember that delicate, succulent taste,
And I'm so glad we didn't pass that shack in our hungry haste -
To find a 'proper modern tea room'
For that afternoon we really were 'over the moon.'

Yes, that was an excellent, simple, tasty meal;
One, often again I'd like to conjure up and make it all real!

Margaret Poole

WHAT IS IT?

A plastic box: with a glass screen
We treat it like a king or queen,
In our sitting rooms it has pride of place
It has moving pictures on its face,
It's one of mankind's most popular means of leisure
We treat it like some valuable treasure,
We can't leave it alone from morn till night
To watch our favourite programmes we'll put up a fight,
It seems to hold us under an hypnotic spell
But it hasn't got me I'm glad to tell,
My husband's one of its multitude of slaves
Sometimes I think this is all he craves,
Sometimes I wonder if he knows I'm there at all
I feel so alone I could climb up the wall,
If only I dare take the fuse out of the plug
Maybe he'd notice me and give me a hug.

C D Kettle

THE ELEPHANT

It is graceful and calm,
gentle yet potent,
it has splendour in itself,
when moving through the dangers of the
hungry world.
It cannot speak, yet its eyes show all
the emotions necessary,
it steadies and protects,
takes pride over young,
but . . . this rare beauty is only deemed
for one purpose:
Death - through destruction.

Louise Jenkins (16)

To Fit In

I sit alone in a dimly lit room
Sweet music fills my ears
I look around the room
And my smile turns to tears
I know I have problems
And habits I must kick
But it's hard staring up from a bottomless pit
Marriage and children fill my friends' lives
While I sit alone and strive
To be with someone instead of alone
To hear her laughter in my empty home
To be able to bear a grin
But most of all to fit in

My life is nothing I took care of that
Alone and disabled that's a fact
Too shy to ask someone to love me
Too scared to take the risk
My heart's filled with love
My lips full of kisses
But all my relationships were misses
I dream of just being held
But when I awake I'm back in my world
Alone confused and sometimes scared
For this world I was not prepared

Tears on my cheeks pain in my heart
My soul naked and bared
I live my existence day by day
But at night I pray
I don't want riches or a life free from sin
My only hope
My only dream is just to fit in

D White

THE WAR IS OVER

The war they say is over,
How we longed for such a day.
The guns have stopped their firing,
the refugees can go back home they say.

To what? No houses just burnt out shells
of the place they once called home.
For their suffering and torture someone
must atone.

The pain etched on their faces tells of
fear beyond belief. Their loved ones
killed, their homes all shelled, who could
deny them some relief.

The war may be over but not in the hearts
of these poor refugees. The scars of grief
stays in their minds, no words can ever ease.
Take heart, we hear your cries, we care and
share with you the pain.

Jill Johnson

SETTING SUN

Watching the colours change,
Seeing faces in the clouds,
I can feel his presence,
I can feel his joy.

It's nearly dark now,
Children have gone in the house,
Reflecting on the busy day,
Helping the homeless,
Trying to make a difference,
With faith, laughter and love.

Kenneth Mood

THE SENTINEL

Immaculate in black he looked,
Surveillance seemed his game
'Twas on TV I saw him,
Though he had no claim to fame.
Quietly watching, waiting
What was it that he sought?
Observing him - so gimlet-eyed,
I had this monstrous thought.
Could he be 'The Harbinger'
Of death, grim reaper's blade,
The silent one to lead us
To pay for sins once made.
Impatience then began to show,
His head moved left and right,
Spine chilling cry was heard by all,
As he prepared for flight.
Off then across the road he went,
To rest at twenty three
Their aerial was just as good,
Relaxed - I then took tea!

T G Bloodworth

THE LAND OF DREAMS

Heroes are strong and extremely bold,
Dragons breathe fire and sleep on gold,
Witches are bad, they're evil as sin,
Wizards are wise but don't always win.
Unicorns are ridden instead of horses,
Trolls and goblins fight the good forces,
Dwarfs against giants, short against tall,
In the Land of Dreams it's one against all.

Mythical beings and talking creatures,
Beautiful heroines with goddess-like features,
Castles and fortresses made of stone,
The good King Ovin sat on his throne,
Princess Elara leading good against bad,
To the dragon's lair where battle is had,
Young Prince Corsen will always win,
In the Land of Dreams, where fantasies begin.

Dominic McDermott

HOLLYWOOD REIGNS, OKAY!

We got into the pictures with a few empty jars.
No nightclubs in those days, no women in bars,
Hollywood made musicals - entertainment was supreme.
Legs like Betty Grable's was every girl's dream.

Carousel, Oklahoma, Annie Get Your Gun,
The endings were the same - romantic hearts were won,
Then came the westerns with Roy Rogers and his trigger,
They changed the scene completely - America seemed bigger.

The simple stories, super songs, the dancing and the stars,
The women all looked glamorous getting into fancy cars.
Now the themes are serious and based upon real life.
There's aye somebody running off with another body's wife.
always someone
The realism, violence and sci-fi movies too
I don't find entertaining - maybe *you* do.
I'd rather see a Fred Astaire or lovely Doris Day
Singing their romantic songs, providing fantasy.
We listened to the
So listen to some music which sent shivers down the spine.
Remember too the organ playing music at half-time.
For folks who led a humdrum life it really was a treat
To sit there in the picture house in a 1/9d seat.

Aileen A Kelly

STAR WALKER . . .

The wheeling universe
crowns me with flaming stars
as I walk the comet dusted
pathway of the heavens . . .

I walk through
gyrating galaxies
as I seek to discover
the far flung frontiers
of our expanding universe.

I move through the macrocosm
getting closer to the boundary
and enter the unknown dimensions
of the cosmic borderline
between the known and the unknown . . .

I am now at the border
of our living universe
which the Prime Mover formed
at the Big Bang explosion
and created in a microsecond.

Does this mean that
beyond our cosmic boundary
there is nothing
no time no space no matter . . .?
Or can it be that beyond our
macrocosmic extremity
that nothing becomes something
when we think quantum thoughts . . . ?

Stephen Gyles

MY FOREVER DREAM

Last night I dreamt that you died in the darkness and
I had not met you in a high up room,
or in a pool we swam
or on a train we travelled.
Then my eyes wet my ears and
it rained on my pillow.

I plugged in the light so I would not picture you
but I saw and I read you
on a page of A4 paper;
the fountain pen cried on,
the clock hand moved forward.
Never having met you
until dreams did us part.

You died in the attic with the stereo playing.
I died in the basement
with your poster falling
from the bare wall and onto the linoleum.
Only a sea but a lifetime apart.

Only the sea but a lifetime apart,
never having known you
until death did us part.

Marie Coghlan

FAITH

I may not understand Him
But He knows what's best for me.
I may not understand Him
But He can see what I can't see.
I may not understand Him
When all my world is caving in.
I may not understand Him
As I struggle with my sin.
I may not understand Him
When I've failed Him once again.
I may not understand Him
As He shares my joy and pain.
I may not understand Him
When my mind is full of doubt.
I may not understand Him
But that's what faith is all about.

Selina Elliott

FAMILY

Your family is the best thing of all,
They're just like a land of gold.
They'll be there, when you need a hand to hold,
Even when you need someone to rely on
Or a shoulder to cry on,
They always think the best of you
And they'll forgive you (whatever you do).
The time you have with them is just great
And they always seem the closest mate.
So you have to tell them how much you care,
Before it's too late,
Because if you lose them,
You'll be in a very bad state.

Abrina Yasin (14)

SUBPOENA TO LIVE

Strolling through life
Loitering, at times
Wandering, like a headless chicken
Surprised by people's capabilities
Deeply inflicted upon
Unable to face the cruelties and injustices
Being slowly attracted towards the tranquillity of
                    isolation -
                              everlasting peace
Feeling the need to heal all pain, to wash it
Away with what droplets of love you have left within
Feeling helpless
Then
Unfeeling
Uncaring
Finally, selfish and frozen.

Sukaina Lyakat Jaffer (18)

DUNGENESS

After a morning of lashing rain
Came a windy afternoon of blue skies.
I set out to drive to Dungeness,
One of my favourite places.
It is the nearest thing to a desert in Britain,
A vast area of shingle ridges
Heaped up by storms and tides over thousands of years,
And jutting out into the English Channel.
Most parts are wild and unspoilt,
Seemingly empty, but hosting many plants and animals,
And hundreds of bird species,
Including migrants attracted by its flooded gravel pits.
I parked my car and walked towards the green and stormy sea.
There, I saw a few anglers, surrounded by fishing tackle, storage
                                                huts and boats;
Old clinker-built wooden boats with little mizzen sails
Contrasting with new ones of fibreglass.
I stayed until grey clouds began massing in the west
Then contentedly returned to my car.
I had seen beauty in bleakness
And in loneliness I had truly felt in communion with nature.

Dorothy Springate

PARA MI MUJERSITA (FOR MY LITTLE WOMAN)

I want to take the pain from you
and give you some respite.
I need to share the bad sensations
to help you win the fight.

I want to tear it from your body
and release it from your mind.
Light the way - show the path
that I so want to find.

With shoulders broad, my arms are strong
so let this be our victory song.
Use my sinews, seize my powers
and let me be your leaning tower.

I want to hear you sing out loud,
to see you run and dance,
I need to pick you from the crowd
oh give me just the chance.

Together we've been all these years
- shared our happiness and our fears,
hold me tight - I will take the strain,
release it now! - We will laugh again.

These pains that dull your eyes are strong
don't suffer alone - that is wrong.
So let it go - give them to me!
And with my strength, we will be free.

William Moyle Breton

A Special Rose

Oh there it is, that special rose,
just a few more days I suppose,
then the colour will be seen,
bursting through those tight green leaves,
what a glorious sight it will be,
this deep red rose my love brings to me,
the first rose of summer, oh no he never forgets,
what a gentle man he is, a love so deep he does confess
and shows it with a warm caress,
I dearly love that man of mine and want to be with him
until the end of time.

Jane Kilsby

DOG'S DINNER

Staunchly lumping inedible status quo
that yanks this poor boy
unhelpfully back from the front row,
Stopping the passionate lad while
angelically screaming in full flow-
We're abysmally verging
on socialism's very unfenced periphery;
Knowing there's no point in even trying
to tie up dangling noose ends:
Tactlessly draped in front
of donkey's mule's eaten carrot -
And then you wonder why
So many
of our gypsy-living type, in bold parentheses,
predictably hit the mildly tempered booze,
Excessively wining
as opposed to dog's dinner dining,
Scrapping backstreet seeking cats and dogs
For first pulsating rummage through trashed litter
To seek out the 'buy one, get one free'
pulse-racing offer of the week.
Retracing one's peppered steps
like the first flag-wielding man on *their* moon;
Compulsively filming
un-dramatic documentary style newsreels
to give ordinary scruffy beings
Some dizzy, dopey spaced-out hope -
Pretty soon.

Stephen Rudd (19)

THE CHANGING AGE

Look back with sadness to the years that have left us,
To the misery of want and the horror of wars,
Remember the miracles science has brought us,
And the changes for good through Parliament's laws.

Look now with anger to the outcome of progress,
To the unjust errors still made by man.
Stamp out the greed and the injustice still with us,
Look forward with hope to the time that must come.

Look out to the future and let us remember,
That the past and the present can teach us to plan
For a future of love and peace and contentment
Through the following of God and the wisdom of man.

A thousand ages, in God's sight
Are, as an evening gone.
Can we, His people, truly feel
We've helped His world along.

Frances Falvey

FAREWELL 20TH CENTURY

Farewell old friend, for time is short
but history shall know your name.
With the suffering in the Balkans
to extinguish your life's flame.
Many tears have fallen,
many have suffered and died.
Families all left homeless,
memories for your final ride.
For into the sunshine of a brand new day
we who are left shall go
loving and caring for each other
that brotherhood may grow.
May poverty never raise its head,
may the hand of friendship be ever strong
turning violence and hatred
into gaiety and song.
May those of different colour and creed
walk hand in hand through life
putting prejudices behind them
through a millennium free from strife.

Victor R A Day

TOWARD 2000

With new Millennium ahead
You, my darling are long dead
I walk toward 2000 year
Thinking shall I leave you here.

'Do you feel the soft wind blow
A presence where so'er you go?
Do you see the moon at night
By the star that shines so bright?

Do you feel me kiss your hand
When by the sea and on the sand?
Do you hear reed-warbler sing
A song of joy to welcome spring?

When life is lightened by a flower
Where I am is where you are.
Don't fear that you will leave me there
For darling, I am always near.

I cannot bear to see you cry
All beings sometime, have to die.
Yet now I know we never leave
Those behind who have to grieve.

While those now dead know of the pain.
But love once felt, is ne'er in vain.
The Wheel of Life is turning. Still
I love you now and always will.'

Anita Richards

TYPICAL WEEKEND IN A PROVINCIAL TOWN?

another weekend
another beating
yet more blood
on the shirt
yet another weekend
of violence
thank God we've got
full employment
(or thereabouts)

yep, it's boredom
again beating
at people's brains
people too busy
destructing
to be
constructing

let's beat each other up
it's so much easier
than thinking
and trying to do
something
about the boredom
around here

P J Gassner

THE PAIN AND HATRED OF LIVING AS ME

I was born, tiny but free
when I opened my eyes
it was love I could see

At first in my cot I learnt how to stand
I took my first step - mummy in hand

Grandad came with us to stay
innocence was taken away
physical, mental, sexual abuse
I was only put here for their use

hurting inside, the pain is real
affection and love I cannot feel

no light in the tunnel that I can see
the pain and hatred of living as me
darkness surrounds, all there is is despair
I'm scared - too scared, but I need to share

searching for comfort, looking for hope
can't take anymore, can no longer cope
overdose swallowed, wrists are slit
legs are cut - the candle's not lit
head is banged, punched 'till I bruise
why don't I die? - I've nothing to lose

hope has gone, far away from me
inside I'm dead - so let me be
no one understands and I can no longer fight
I surrender to the pain - there is no light.

Valerie Gibson

MY GRANNY

I open the door
A pong hits my face
A narky old woman
Sits in a pool of no disgrace.

Grease in her hair
A fag in her hand
A whiskey beside her
'Tis her choice to despair.

Misery surrounds her
Servants dance round her
She'll smoke non-stop
Until she pops.

She needs a good bath
And a pad down below
But she's that stubborn
She won't go.

One day I will find her
Stone cold in the bed
A drink and a fag
Has gone yet away.

Andrea McLoughlin

TO MY LOVE

I stood with you one happy sunlit day
Upon a tiny bridge o'er rippling stream
And told you of my love
'Neath sky serene.
A silver wingèd seagull soared above
And trees made silhouettes against the blue
Where clouds were drifting by
And then I knew -
As long as nature's wings caress the earth
And springtime's young green leaves are bathed in dew,
As long as there is life
I'll cherish you.

Betty Bevan

WORLD TO LET

To let - a mature residence with character and style,
has been neglected lately and in need of some repairs,
ideally suited for contact with the universe around,
a good home waiting for someone who really cares.

The grounds need to be landscaped and trees to be replaced,
the pond life has depleted and needs to be restocked,
that nature sanctuary to be retained as a home for wildlife,
the dwelling needs an airing with all the doors unlocked.

It's quite an imposing task to undertake, I must agree,
but the potential there is huge for anyone with time to spare,
time to see the beauty of the mountains, fields and streams,
and the will to work with diligence to preserve the beauty there.

To let, free of charge, all comers are considered,
no references required - any colour, race or creed,
anyone who seeks adventure that will bring its own reward
please apply at once, your commitment's all we need.

Ann Rutherford

YOU ARE STANDING ON MY POEM

Spring is a time of renewal.
But last year's brown
Lie sideways in clusters
Relics of the past
Dry and springless.

Mirrors, all of these children
Leaves returning every year
Perfectly formed
Identical; clones.
Only we change.

Stephen Misner

CATS

I hate cats
Miaowing, malevolent, marauding, malicious
Waving their tails ferociously
Stalking - proud as kings
As though the world belonged to them
And we their hirelings
They use our softest seat like thrones;
Stretching their cruel claws
Purring secret wickedness
Behind those spiteful paws
Many people love cats
Why? I cannot see,
I hate cats.
Cats hate me.

C A Harrison

TAIG

Calls out in anger
Abuse to men or women
Need to take me as I am
Taig something in Irish

Diving for cover a translation
Rely on the word of the Lord
All men are equal
In the sight of God

Catholic in Belfast abused
France, Italy no sin
To be Catholic, a good woman
People shout out *Taig*

S M Thompson

JUST A POET

If you know of a poet it may well be someone who is
in some ways disorganised.
For having to wait for inspiration, unlike elements of a trade,
poetic origination cannot be analysed.
Ideas often come at unsociable times, perhaps in the
middle of the night.
And there will be many drafts to follow so as to get it right.
With a trade, there are rules and regulations from which
we can rarely deviate.
Whereas with rhyme we can be unconventional, not having to relate.
If you have been an engineer and become a poet, you can appreciate
the freedom to express.
That was not there when having to conform, but there's a need
to control emotions nonetheless.
For some subjects are controversial calling for a diplomatic approach
- to say the least.
In fact some writers overstep the mark and are branded as a beast.
There are many delicate occasions when we insist our words are
'Tongue in cheek'
And a certain poetic licence is allowed always taking care
not to offend before we speak.
As a poet all of this must be accountable before words
are committed to rhyme.
So it follows that to be a poet is more complex than was perhaps
thought with so much to consider all the time.

Reg Morris

THE TOY CUPBOARD

Rupert, a rash Teddy Bear,
Would do anything for a dare.
One day, when in debt,
He accepted a bet,
And went and shaved off all his hair.

The Fairy Doll shared a close bond
With her friends splashing round in the pond.
Then one jerked her head
And pointedly said,
'Take care what you do with that wand!'

Thomas, who'd got a new kite,
Attempted to fly it at night.
It was then that a freak
Lightning streak
Set Thomas's new kite alight.

The Toy Soldiers stood on parade,
In tunics and bearskins arrayed.
But they went back to bed
When the Field Marshal said,
'There's no war today, I'm afraid.'

Frank Jensen

My Beloved Sweetpea

I hear your voice in some far off dreamland
Reaching out our hands almost touch
As we laugh and play together once again
The sun's always shining, never a drop of rain
Sandcastles built in clouds on high
Rivers made up of tears
These seven years, I have cried rush on by
I can see your special smile
The sun that shone so bright in our lives
The flower that really had no time to reach full bloom
Your petals crushed by evil hands
How I love our time together in that dreamland
I only wish I could hold you there
But each time Grandad says it's time to go
For me it's not time
So to this land I return, my heart still bursting
With love for you,
Some love goes beyond the grave
My love for you is eternal, forever and a day
As only a mother's love can be
In a unique and special way.

Kathleen Lunnon

THE NATURAL WORLD

Ever omnipotent
Extends her invitation
To view - the symmetry
Of life
As witnessed when
The sun's orb
Casting an illusory spell
O'er sparkling waters
Delivers a oneness
To the guest.

Irene Gunnion

AMPHIPOD - THE SAND HOPPER

Amphipod, amphipod, where have you been?
I have been to see Neptune about keeping the seas clean.
Amphipod, amphipod, what did he say?
He told me to keep on doing it my way.
Amphipod, amphipod, how is it done?
I gather dead bits to stuff in my tum.
Amphipod, amphipod, what gives you pains?
All the nasty chemicals man pours down his drains.
Amphipod, amphipod, what happens to you?
I get eaten by fishes who are then eaten by you!

A E Joyce

FRIENDS

The aches and pains all over me
Right from my ankle past my knee
Keeps me awake most of the night
Take a tablet hope to put it right

At last the sleep I want has come
I wake up to the morning sun
Today I hope will be less pain
And I will be able to walk again

Good friends I have who really care
One is even going to do my hair
So even if you're not too well
Your true friends you can tell.

J Christensen

ANGRY MODE

The red mist descends and you then explode,
You've spat the dummy and have blown,
That excess of testosterone,
You've gone to meltdown way past overload,
Get out of my way you're in my road,
It's happened before and you should have known,
Those temper tantrums you should have outgrown,
A shameful example of 'Angry Mode'
What do others think when you rant and rave?
It's the wrong way to get my compliance,
If a child would result in you getting smacked,
It's the way spoilt children misbehave,
You may find me snarling in defiance,
This knee jerk way that you always react.

John Smurthwaite

THE COPPER BEECH TREE

The copper beech tree has stood there,
For more years than we seem to care,
Bark gnarled and rugged, like an old man,
Picture its quality if you can.

Its leaves they shine with russet gold,
The magnificent beauty could not be told,
You had to see with your own eyes,
This regal splendour against the skies.

Branches spread like angels' wings,
Safe haven for birds and other things,
But now it's dying, it's no use crying,
The time has come, its life is done.

It's our own fault - but we still can't see,
The damage we are doing to this tree.
With fossil fuels and acid rain,
No wonder it is racked with pain.

In come the men with their chainsaws,
And tear its limbs without a pause,
Slice by slice they drop with a thump,
Leaving nothing but a stump.

And now it's gone forever more,
My sadness great, my heart is sore,
For my children will never see,
The beauty of that old *beech tree*.

Winnie Gordon

DIANA . . . OUR BEAUTIFUL PRINCESS

Oh, Diana, our beautiful Princess,
who's been castigated for going astray,
would you have taken that wrongful road
if with you, your spouse did not deceitfully play.

Half the world did think you a Saint,
half the world thought you a sinner:
But there are many hypocrites in the world,
you, beautiful Princess, could never be the winner.

You cuddled the sick, both black and white,
always knowing you were doing right:
You travelled worldwide, not for the rides
but to nurse darkened lives, giving them light.

Many folk were jealous of your beauty and grace,
they felt they had lost the popularity race,
so out came the knives for stabs in the back -
oh, what a pity we disposed of the rack!

But, beautiful Princess, whose life was cut short,
worry not that people jeer and snort:
You have gone from us to another life
and to receive from Him - His Love, not strife.

Peace be with you.

Geo K Phillips

IF I WERE OF

If I were of a lesser specie
Less conscious of my existence
Of plagues, gnaws, doubts and fears
And no knowledge of persistence

Accepting things the way they are
No reflection on tomorrow
Akin of food and reproduction
No ken of joy or sorrow

No doubt a predator I'd be
Upon others of my kind,
And then again perhaps a prey
With action unrefined

Who knows what my environment
Be it earth or sea or where
Or an animal's intestine
Having no need or air

Perhaps no brain just a single nerve
Controlling my meagre lifestyle
Life span of perhaps a month
Or less in environs hostile

I'd have no need of fol de rols
Or goods of any kind
Just the bare necessities
Mainly food to find

Of what will have been my purpose
The mystery will ne'er unfold
Perhaps to control the lives of others
Or to increase my kind tenfold.

Jardun

CLOSE OF DAY

Midnight chimes from a distant street.
Frail hands clutching at empty straws.
The echo of steps from weary feet.
Darkness looming as daylight goes.

O'er the dark forest glades
The moon sheds its light,
As day quickly fades
To the silence of the night.

From a sleeping world
All grey mists now gone.
Bringing comfort and hope
To greet a new dawn.

Sophia D Winchester

THE ORANGE DAY STAR

You make me happy, you are my joy
You are my man, you are my boy.
My orange day star,
My elegant tsar.

My orange day star you are far from me,
Yet you make me happy.
My orange day star grow close
For my love for you is grandiose.

Orange, red and yellow sparkle within your soul,
Take me close beside you; that is my role.
Hand in hand forever with you near,
For you know how much I hold you dear.

Denise Shaw

EMPTY

Empty space inside of me, feels like someone died.
Unfulfilled, dissatisfied, can no longer hide.
Light another cigarette, fill the vacant space.
Glimpsed the haunted eyes in my expressionless face.

Empty space inside of me, black cloud of depression.
Child within an adult, afraid of my regression.
Binge-vomit cycle, desperate need to feel whole.
Somehow lost my way, a fruitless search for soul.

Empty space inside of me, please make it go away.
Detached and disconnected, nothing left to say.
Reach for the bottle, numbness blocks the pain.
Empty life and loneliness driving me insane.

Leila Brewer

AS WE ARE MARCHING ALONG

We act as a group, and we feel so strong.
No one should be in our ways,
When we are jointly marching along,
With a common faith and a common song,
To demonstrate our case.
The others are different, that is their lack;
They might be yellow or brown,
They might be white, or they might be black
Or just from another town.
Because they are different, *they* must be blamed!
The truth is on *our* side.
So *they* must be wrong and should feel ashamed.
We have the eternal right,
That says the guru, who thinks for us.
He says, what we ought to believe,
And what he says, we will not discuss,
As he ensures us: we will receive,
What we are entitled to get and possess,
If we strictly follow his rule.
Whatever we do, he will sanction and bless,
As we are his weapon and tool.
No doubt is ever on our mind,
That what we were doing was wrong.
We leave all thinking and feeling behind,
As we are marching along.
And the strong words turn into fire and sword,
When we cross our borderline.
And the others will suffer and will be taught,
What it means to be different from *our* design.
And we burn their temple and take their land,
And cleanse from that vermin the place.

And if they suffered from our hand
And perished all in that blaze,
It would be *their* fault, if they fell and died!
Why don't they want to belong
To the men, who have the truth on their side
And the proper faith and immortal right
And who are so determined and strong,
When they are marching along!

Henning Nolte

PLASTIC DESTINY

Why an artificial noun
multicoloured, multi-lingual, multi-purpose
even multi-storied . . .
many faces, many facets, many guises
like a bowl, brush, comb, cassette-case
deodorant, flower vase, dustpan and brush
pedal-bin, swing-bin, litter bin
I wear a mask in this plastic world
longing like Eleanor Rigby for reality
once put before an oil-painting I owned obscurity
paled into insignificance, paled like faded wallpaper
that everyone forgets until needed
my destiny is only a recycling box like me
hollow, mundane, artificial
untreasured like a crystal cut-glass vase
another noun, dead existence lives on
until I have served my purpose
to hug living daffodils, to contain water,
wash the wear and tear from weary feet
crying inside for recognition
like the portrait painted oil
in pride of place over mantelpiece.
Onyx statues starkly cold in contrast
and the round glided clock mocks me
silvery spoons, knives, forks catch candlelit golden glow
reflecting in white wine glasses and clear blue crockery
I am a wine bottle opener; here for a transitory time
of vague nostalgia and euphoric energy.

Shall I say grace, give thanks
for being a broom, brush, handle
recognition eludes me; an ephemeral existence
a transitory toy; a yellow submarine
a Fisher-Price label, pleasurable plastic . . .

I just want to be myself,
discard this mediocre mask of unreality

But . . . what is the real thing in life's incessant quest
will my restless test be rewarded
in the recycling bin?

And what is the *real* thing? Pepsi? Or Coke?

Judy Studd

COME ON, BRING IN THE NEWS

Not another poem
Taking up space
Relegate is somewhere
Anywhere will do,
Substitute a cartoon,
Go for reaction,
We want action
Only prose will do,
Come on, bring in the news.

Patrick Cooper-Duffy

ELIJAH'S CLOUD

First a wisp of cloud in all that blue!
And the nearest hills look sunnier than before,
The yellow fields begin to look brand-new,
Then turn dark green beyond the valley door;
And hawthorns lose their spread of red and white,
And woods and trees turn khaki in the day.

And though the day is far from evening light,
A darkness spreads in clouds of mist and spray,
And the little cloud is joined by clouds in flight,
Some black, some white, with tops of bluish-grey;
And the rain in sheets - swirls all the way to the ground,
From stratocumuli and nebulae below.

And the larger trees sway heavy in the wind,
And the valley smokes with water high and low,
And in shafts of light - a rainbow from behind,
Deeper than I've ever cared to know;
And the rain then fills up every brook and road,
With all the drains and culverts quickly filled.

Tom Ritchie

AUTUMN

A lacy spider's web between dewy long-grassed blades
Shivering sun-sparked in early morning breeze
Sprays of ripe bramble-fruit on the hedge
And shiny conkers plopping from the trees
Mist at morn' and thin blue haze throughout the day
Red berries thick upon leaf-dropping thorn
Yet stubbled fields from sun-ripened corn
Bud and flower of rose still in bright array
Majestic coppered mantle of the towering beech
Noble spreading oak still clad in khaki green
Warm the mellowed brick which holds the peach
Bowed the pear and apple yet to glean
Somnolent the day ere bright moonlight
To glitter, glisten on the murmuring stream
And bathe the fields in soft nocturnal gleam
Then hide cloud-covered out of sight
Gorgeous sunsets with deep pastel hues
No sign of hard weather duck-egg blue
Vibrant still the flowers of summertime
Seed from burst pods to fruit where spreading flew
Heather blooms and bees still restless toil
Russet bracken humbled from once proud display
Down of late thistle floats vaguely through the air
Birds sunbathe and lazy doze the hours away
Skittish touch of cooler air to swirl the dust
Splash of droplets from sullen copper sky
Crazed the ant in seeming restless search
Fretful the wasp and stir of boughs in gentle sigh
What say the chirping sparrows on sun-warmed roof
Just that autumn days are drifting by.

G Stribling

SUBMISSIONS INVITED
SOMETHING FOR EVERYONE.

POETRY NOW '99 - Any subject,
any style, any time.

WOMENSWORDS '99 - Strictly women,
have your say the female way!

STRONGWORDS '99 - Warning!
Age restriction, must be between 16-24,
opinionated and have strong views.
(Not for the faint-hearted)

All poems no longer than 30 lines.
Always welcome! No fee!
Cash Prizes to be won!

Mark your envelope (eg *Poetry Now) '99*
Send to:
Forward Press Ltd
Remus House, Coltsfoot Drive,
Woodston,
Peterborough, PE2 9JX

OVER £10,000 POETRY PRIZES
TO BE WON!

Judging will take place in October 1999